Literature Circle Guide:

Bud, Not Buddy

by Kathy Pounds

New York • **Toronto** • **London** • **Auckland** • **Sydney**
• **Mexico City** • **New Delhi** • **Hong Kong** • **Buenos Aires**

Guide written by Kathy Pounds
Edited by Sarah Glasscock
Cover design by Niloufar Safavieh
Interior design by Grafica, Inc.
Interior illustrations by Mona Mark

Credits: Cover: Jacket cover for BUD, NOT BUDDY by Christopher Paul Curtis. Used by permission of Random House Children's Books, a division of Random House, Inc. Interior: Author photo on page 9 by James Keyser/Random House Children's Books.

ISBN 0-439-35534-6

2 3 4 5 6 7 8 9 10   40   08 07 06 05 04 03 02

Contents

To the Teacher

As a teacher, you naturally want to instill in your students the habits of confident, critical, independent, and lifelong readers. You hope that even when students are not in school they will seek out books on their own, think about and question what they are reading, and share those ideas with friends. An excellent way to further this goal is by using literature circles in your classroom.

In a literature circle, students select a book to read as a group. They think and write about it on their own in a literature response journal, and then discuss it together. Both journals and discussions enable students to respond to a book and develop their insights into it. They also learn to identify themes and issues, analyze vocabulary, recognize writing techniques, and share ideas with each other—all of which are necessary to meet state and national standards.

This guide provides the support materials for using literature circles with *Bud, Not Buddy* by Christopher Paul Curtis. The reading strategies, discussion questions, projects, and enrichment readings will also support a whole class reading of this text or can be given to enhance the experience of an individual student reading the book as part of a reading workshop.

Literature Circles

A literature circle consists of several students (usually three to five) who agree to read a book together and share their observations, questions, and interpretations. Groups may be organized by reading level or choice of book. Often these groups read more than one book together since, as students become more comfortable talking with one another, their observations and insights deepen.

When planning to use literature circles in your classroom, it can be helpful to do the following:

✳ Recommend four or five books from which students can choose. These books might be grouped by theme, genre, or author.

✳ Allow three or four weeks for students to read each book. Each of Scholastic's *Literature Circle Guides* has the same number of sections as well as enrichment activities and projects. Even if students are reading different books in the *Literature Circle Guide* series, they can be scheduled to finish at the same time.

✳ Create a daily routine so students can focus on journal writing and discussions.

✳ Decide whether students will be reading books in class or for homework. If students do all their reading for homework, then allot class time for sharing journals and discussions. You can also alternate silent reading and writing days in the classroom with discussion groups.

Read More About Literature Circles

Getting the Most from Literature Groups by Penny Strube (Scholastic Professional Books, 1996)

Literature Circles by Harvey Daniels (Stenhouse Publishers, 1994)

Using the *Literature Circle Guides* in Your Classroom

Each guide contains the following sections:

* ❋ background information about the author and book
* ❋ enrichment readings relevant to the book
* ❋ Literature Response Journal reproducibles
* ❋ Group Discussion reproducibles
* ❋ Individual and group projects
* ❋ Literature Discussion Evaluation Sheet

Background Information and Enrichment Readings

The background information about the author and the book and the enrichment readings are designed to offer information that will enhance students' understanding of the book. You may choose to assign and discuss these sections before, during, or after the reading of the book. Because each enrichment concludes with questions that invite students to connect it to the book, you can use this section to inspire them to think and record their thoughts in the literature response journal.

Literature Response Journal Reproducibles

Although these reproducibles are designed for individual students, they should also be used to stimulate and support discussions in literature circles. Each page begins with a reading strategy and follows with several journal topics. At the bottom of the page, students select a type of response (prediction, question, observation, or connection) for free-choice writing in their response journals.

◆ Reading Strategies

Since the goal of the literature circle is to empower lifelong readers, a different reading strategy is introduced in each section. Not only does the reading strategy allow students to understand this particular book better, it also instills a habit of mind that will continue to be useful when they read other books. A question from the Literature Response Journal and the Group Discussion pages is always tied to the reading strategy.

If everyone in class is reading the same book, you may present the reading strategy as a mini-lesson to the entire class. For literature circles, however, the group of students can read over and discuss the strategy together at the start of class and then experiment with the strategy as they read silently for the rest of the period. You may want to allow time at the end of class so the group can talk about what they noticed as they read. As an alternative, the literature circle can review the reading strategy for the next section after they have completed their discussion. That night, students can try out the reading strategy as they read on their own so they will be ready for the next day's literature circle discussion.

◆ Literature Response Journal Topics

A literature response journal allows a reader to "converse" with a book. Students write questions, point out things they notice about the story, recall personal experiences, and make connections to other texts in their journals. In other words, they are using writing to explore what they think about the book. See page 7 for tips on how to help students set up their literature response journals.

1. The questions for the literature response journals have no right or wrong answers but are designed to help students look beneath the surface of the plot and develop a richer connection to the story and its characters.

2. Students can write in their literature response journals as soon as they have finished a reading assignment. Again, you may choose to have students do this for homework or make time during class.

3. The literature response journals are an excellent tool for students to use in their literature circles. They can highlight ideas and thoughts in their journals that they want to share with the group.

4. When you evaluate students' journals, consider whether they have completed all the assignments and have responded in depth and thoughtfully. You may want to check each day to make sure students are keeping up with the assignments. You can read and respond to the journals at a halfway point (after five entries) and again at the end. Some teachers suggest that students pick out their five best entries for a grade.

Group Discussion Reproducibles

These reproducibles are designed for use in literature circles. Each page begins with a series of discussion questions for the group to consider. A mini-lesson on an aspect of the writer's craft follows the discussion questions. See page 8 for tips on how to model good discussions for students.

◆ **Literature Discussion Questions:** In a literature discussion, students experience a book from different points of view. Each reader brings her or his own unique observations, questions, and associations to the text. When students share their different reading experiences, they often come to a wider and deeper understanding than they would have reached on their own.

The discussion is not an exercise in finding the right answers nor is it a debate. Its goal is to explore the many possible meanings of a book. Be sure to allow enough time for these conversations to move beyond easy answers—try to schedule 25–35 minutes for each one. In addition, there are important guidelines to ensure that everyone's voice is heard.

1. Let students know that participation in the literature discussion is an important part of their grade. You may choose to watch one discussion and grade it. (You can use the Literature Discussion Evaluation Sheet on page 33.)

2. Encourage students to evaluate their own performance in discussions using the Literature Discussion Evaluation Sheet. They can assess not only their own level of involvement but also how the group itself has functioned.

3. Help students learn how to talk to one another effectively. After a discussion, help them process what worked and what didn't. Videotape discussions if possible, and then evaluate them together. Let one literature circle watch another and provide feedback to it.

4. It can be helpful to have a facilitator for each discussion. The facilitator can keep students from interrupting each other, help the conversation get back on track when it digresses, and encourage shyer members to contribute. At the end of each discussion, the facilitator can summarize everyone's contributions and suggest areas for improvement.

5. Designate other roles for group members. For instance, a recorder can take notes and/or list questions for further discussion. A summarizer can open each literature circle meeting by summarizing the chapter(s) the group has just read. Encourage students to rotate these roles, as well as that of the facilitator.

◆ **The Writer's Craft:** This section encourages students to look at the writer's most important tool—words. It points out new vocabulary, writing techniques, and uses of language. One or two questions invite students to think more deeply about the book and writing in general. These questions can either become part of the literature circle discussion or be written about in students' journals.

Literature Discussion Evaluation Sheet

Both you and your students will benefit from completing these evaluation sheets. You can use them to assess students' performance, and as mentioned earlier, students can evaluate their own individual performances, as well as their group's performance. The Literature Discussion Evaluation Sheet appears on page 33.

Setting Up Literature Response Journals

Although some students may already keep literature response journals, others may not know how to begin. To discourage students from merely writing elaborate plot summaries and to encourage them to use their journals in a meaningful way, help them focus their responses around the following elements: predictions, observations, questions, and connections. Have students take time after each assigned section to think about and record their responses in their journals. Sample responses appear below.

◆ **Predictions:** Before students read the book, have them study the cover and the jacket copy. Ask if anyone has read another book by Christopher Paul Curtis. To begin their literature response journals, tell students to jot down their impressions about the book. As they read, students will continue to make predictions about what a character might do or how the plot might turn. After finishing the book, students can re-assess their initial predictions. Good readers understand that they must constantly activate prior knowledge before, during, and after they read. They adjust their expectations and predictions; a book that is completely predictable is not likely to capture anyone's interest. A student about to read *Bud, Not Buddy* for the first time might predict the following:

> *When I looked at the cover, I thought the boy was dreaming about becoming a musician. Then I read that Bud ran away to look for his father, so he must have been thinking about his dad. He must be a lot braver than most ten year olds!*

◆ **Observations:** This activity takes place immediately after reading begins. In a literature response journal, the reader recalls fresh impressions about the characters, setting, and events. Most readers mention details that stand out for them even if they are not sure what their importance is. For example, a reader might list phrases that describe how a character looks or the feeling a setting evokes. Many readers note certain words, phrases, or passages in a book.

Others note the style of an author's writing or the voice in which the story is told. A student just starting to read *Bud, Not Buddy* might write the following:

> *I felt sorry for Bud when he said he was going to his third foster home. He must not expect it to work because he said, "Here we go again." I was surprised that he tried to make Jerry feel better. Most people would just think of themselves.*

◆ **Questions:** Point out that good readers don't necessarily understand everything they read. To clarify their uncertainty, they ask questions. Encourage students to identify passages that confuse or trouble them and emphasize that they shouldn't take anything for granted. Share the following student example:

> *What does Miss Thomas mean when she tells Bud he's a godsend? Is that good? Why should he think about that all the time?*

◆ **Connections:** Remind students that one story often leads to another. When one friend tells a story, the other friend is often inspired to tell one too. The same thing happens when someone reads a book. A character reminds the reader of a relative, or a situation is similar to something that happened to him or her. Sometimes a book makes a reader recall other books or movies. These connections can be helpful in revealing some of the deeper meanings or patterns of a book. The following is an example of a student connection:

> *The title makes me think of my friend Christopher. He doesn't like anybody calling him "Squirt." I used to think he was too sensitive about it. Now that I think about it, I wouldn't like anybody making up a name for me—especially if it felt like people were using it to make fun of me .*

The Good Discussion

In a good literature discussion, students are always learning from one another. They listen to one another and respond to what their peers have to say. They share their ideas, questions, and observations. Everyone feels comfortable about talking, and no one interrupts or puts down what anyone else says. Students leave a good literature discussion with a new understanding of the book—and sometimes with new questions about it. They almost always feel more engaged by what they have read.

◆ **Modeling a Good Discussion:** In this era of combative and confessional TV talk shows, students often don't have any idea of what it means to talk productively and creatively together. You can help them have a better idea of what a good literature discussion is if you let them experience one. Select a thought-provoking short story or poem for students to read, and then choose a small group to model a discussion of the work for the class.

Explain to participating students that the objective of the discussion is to explore the text thoroughly and learn from one another. Emphasize that it takes time to learn how to have a good discussion, and that the first discussion may not achieve everything they hope it will. Duplicate a copy of the Literature Discussion Evaluation Sheet for each student. Go over the helpful and unhelpful contributions shown on it. Instruct students to fill out the sheet as they watch the model discussion. Then have the group of students hold its discussion while the rest of the class observes. Try not to interrupt or control the discussion and remind the student audience not to participate. It's okay if the discussion falters, as this is a learning experience.

Allow 15–20 minutes for the discussion. When it is finished, ask each student in the group to reflect out loud about what worked and what didn't. Then have the students who observed share their impressions. What kinds of comments were helpful? How could the group have talked to each other more productively? You may want to let another group experiment with a discussion so students can try out what they learned from the first one.

◆ **Assessing Discussions:** The following tips will help students monitor how well their group is functioning:

1. One person should keep track of all behaviors by each group member, both helpful and unhelpful, during the discussion.

2. At the end of the discussion, each individual should think about how he or she did. How many helpful and unhelpful checks did he or she receive?

3. The group should look at the Literature Discussion Evaluation Sheet and assess their performance as a whole. Were most of the behaviors helpful? Were any behaviors unhelpful? How could the group improve?

In good discussions, you will often hear students say the following:

"I was wondering if anyone knew . . ."

"I see what you are saying. That reminds me of something that happened earlier in the book."

"What do you think?"

"Did anyone notice on page 57 that . . ."

"I disagree with you because . . ."

"I agree with you because . . ."

"This reminds me so much of when . . ."

"Do you think this could mean . . ."

"I'm not sure I understand what you're saying. Could you explain it a little more to me?"

"That reminds me of what you were saying yesterday about . . ."

"I just don't understand this."

"I love the part that says . . ."

"Here, let me read this paragraph. It's an example of what I'm talking about."

About *Bud, Not Buddy*

Winner of the Newbery Medal and the Coretta Scott King Award, *Bud, Not Buddy* is the story of a young boy who lives a kid's worst nightmare—he's homeless; his mother is dead; and his father's identity is uncertain. But Bud is tough. He handles difficulties with humor and never runs out of hope and perseverance. He's independent, yet accepts the kindness of strangers. He shows us that although we belong to the family of man, there's something special about the family we're born into. As Christopher Paul Curtis put it, "When you stop to think about it, everything is about trying to find somewhere you belong."

About the Author: Christopher Paul Curtis

Unlike Bud, Christopher Paul Curtis does know where he belongs. He grew up in Flint, Michigan, with parents he describes as great readers, active in the civil rights movement, and relatively strict by today's standards. He and his four brothers and sisters knew the rules they had to follow, what they had to do, and what was expected of them.

Although his parents encouraged him to read and supported his interest in drama—he acted in summer theater in Flint as a child and toured Europe with a theater troupe when he was eighteen—Curtis followed his own mind when it was time to make decisions about what he wanted to do. Instead of finishing a college degree right out of high school, he started working at the Fisher Body Plant, hanging eighty-pound car doors on Buicks, ten hours a day for twelve years.

Eventually, Curtis found he hated the assembly line. Reading and writing became his lifeline. He escaped boredom at work by reading or writing during breaks. He went to school at night and worked on his degree. Finally, with the encouragement of his wife, Curtis left his job and began writing full-time. Later he worked at odd jobs to earn money for his family and spent mornings writing in longhand at the Children's Room of the Windsor, Ontario, public library.

Curtis uses his varied life experiences in his writing. "I get my ideas from things that have happened to me, things that I find interesting, things that happen to other people."

Although he wasn't a big reader when he was young, Mr. Curtis now calls himself a binge reader and reads anything that has a good story. When he's not reading or writing, he spends time with his wife, son, and daughter, helps with housework, plays basketball three times a week, and listens to music—often one of the 2,500 record albums he's collected.

What advice does Mr. Curtis have for writers? "Just start the story somewhere. Just think of a conversation. Think of something that was going on. That's what I would do with Bud. It's a long process. It's like getting to know somebody.

"Write anytime you have the opportunity. Set up particular times everyday when you write and stick to the schedule. I think writing is like any other skill, you have to practice. It's like an instrument or sport."

Other Books by Christopher Paul Curtis

The Watsons Go to Birmingham—1963

Enrichment: Life in the 30s

The Great Depression that began in 1929 changed life for almost everyone in the United States. By 1932, nearly 85,000 businesses had failed, and 5,000 banks had closed. A quarter of the population was unemployed, and among those who did have jobs, many only worked part-time. African Americans were especially hard hit—at least half were unemployed. Society was segregated, and competition for work was stiff. In those hard times, African Americans were often the last hired and first fired.

As the Depression deepened, people of all races and economic levels had trouble paying their bills, buying food, and keeping a roof over their heads. Farmers, who were usually self-sufficient, suffered from natural disasters and low crop prices; their income was only one-third what it was in 1929. The half of the U.S. population that lived in the cities often couldn't pay for food grown by the farmers, yet they had no way to grow their own. By 1933, a million people were reduced to living in Hoovervilles, or shantytowns, and scrounging for their daily needs. Others called hoboes took to the roads or rails looking for work. Whole families moved around, as did teenagers and children, who traveled together in small groups for safety.

In 1936, the year in which *Bud, Not Buddy* is set, people had begun to have some hope. President Franklin Delano Roosevelt had started New Deal programs designed to ease the suffering of millions. In addition, the National Labor Relations Act had passed, which was legislation that allowed workers to form unions and negotiate for better working conditions and higher pay. While these programs made life better, the suffering was not over until the Depression ended with the beginning of World War II.

To distract them from their daily concerns during the Depression, families enjoyed inexpensive entertainment. At home, they played bridge, chess, card games, and Monopoly. They read. Home subscriptions to newspapers went down, but public library use went up. The most popular books were *The Good Earth*, *Anthony Adverse*, and *Gone With the Wind*. Kids read comics, such as Blondie, Dick Tracy, L'il Abner, and Popeye the Sailor. They listened to radio, an integral part of the day for millions. They heard President Roosevelt's fireside chats, programs like "Amos and Andy" and "Amateur Hour," and the music of Rudy Vallee and Kate Smith. Not surprisingly, "Brother, Can You Spare a Dime?" was the song most often sung. Radio even perked up the earnings of major league baseball. Team revenues were down until radio stations bought broadcast rights for games.

Two of the biggest forms of entertainment outside the home were miniature golf and movies. For only 15 cents, families might golf at one of 30,000 miniature courses, and for about the same price, children and adults could forget their worries at a movie theater. More than 60 million tickets were sold each week for movies like *King Kong*, *Little Women*, and *The Thin Man*. It was the heyday of Shirley Temple, Clark Gable, Paul Robeson, and Oscar Micheaux's "race" movies that featured all African-American casts.

These facts provide only a general impression of life during the Great Depression. What details are missing? What questions would you like to ask a person who lived during this time? Although *Bud, Not Buddy* is fiction, what does it add to what you know about the Depression? How does the book deepen your understanding of that time?

Enrichment: Jazz

To understand jazz—the music that was popular in the 1920s and 1930s—it helps to know about the musical traditions from which jazz grew. Its earliest roots are in the community music that was part of African daily life. Moving in time to the pounding rhythm of drums, members of a community would dance, sing and clap, improvising and interacting with a leader in what came to be known as "call and response." In contrast, European music was written down, involved the blending of complex harmonies, and was performed by an individual or group for the rest of the community.

In the United States before the Civil War, slaves combined the music they brought from Africa, the European-based music they heard from their owners, and the music they heard as they moved from one plantation to another. After the Civil War, when African Americans could travel more freely, the exchange and interweaving of music intensified.

In New York, early jazz was played by large dance orchestras with violins, cellos, mandolins, and pianos—instruments mostly popular with European orchestras. During World War I, the best African-American military band toured Europe, playing jazz there for the first time. Later, large dance bands like Duke Ellington's played at the Cotton Club and other nightclubs. African Americans could not attend the nightclubs and instead hosted "rent" parties, get-togethers for which participants paid a small admission fee for the services of a good piano player. Fats Waller was a famous composer and pianist who got his start this way.

The jazz that developed in New Orleans grew out of the mix of cultures that settled there—French, Spanish, African, Native American, and European. Early brass bands brought in by the French played marches, polkas, and waltzes, and in time, evolved into the African-American bands of the 20th century that became famous for their mournful funeral dirges. Unlike European orchestral music, music for these bands was not written down and players could improvise; a song would be different every time it was played.

During Prohibition (1920–1933), Chicago became the center of the jazz world. Many jazz musicians moved there from New Orleans to play at the speakeasies, or clubs that opened because the ban on alcohol was not enforced as strenuously as in other cities. In Chicago, jazz was called "hot." Long, improvised solos played on drums, piano, string bass, and saxophone became important. Louis Armstrong, famous for his trumpet solos, became the first to "scat" sing or use his voice to make sounds like an instrument. Armstrong also was known for the play between his trumpet and the piano, a return to the "call and response" of earlier days.

In the 1930s, a type of jazz called "swing" became popular. Big bands played smooth, rehearsed music with less improvisation. Words could be put to this kind of music, and women singers such as Billie Holiday frequently accompanied the bands. Also musicians often played music written by others. Fletcher Henderson, a classical musician and the director of Black Swan, the first African-American owned record company, wrote orchestral arrangements for players such as Louis Armstrong and Benny Goodman.

Although the big bands and famous musicians mostly played in large cities, smaller bands like Herman E. Calloway's in *Bud, Not Buddy* brought the sounds of jazz and swing to small towns across America.

What do you learn about the life of the small traveling band in *Bud, Not Buddy*? What are the challenges and rewards of such a life? Why do you think the music and life with the band appealed to Bud?

Enrichment: Pullman Porters

In the 1930s, when you traveled somewhere far from home, you would probably take the train. The Pullman porters on the train would make your journey comfortable.

Before 1869, overnight train travel wasn't very pleasant. Twenty-five to forty passengers would sit on straight-backed, hard wooden benches in an unheated or unair-conditioned coach. There were no bathrooms, and no dining cars or snack bars from which to buy food. The men who traveled on trains were so rough that women demanded separate cars. For many years, some wealthy riders bought private cars that were then hitched to regular trains.

This all changed in 1863 when George Pullman built an impressive new sleeping car called the *Pioneer*. It incorporated black walnut wood, elegant chandeliers, comfortable seats, rich carpeting, good linens, and marble washstands. After the end of the Civil War and the completion of the transcontinental railroad in 1869, Pullman's cars were in demand by railroad companies wanting to expand their passenger services. He supplied both the cars and the staff for them. Pullman built his reputation on luxurious cars and first-class service.

To staff his cars, Pullman hired former slaves who didn't have many work options after the Civil War. Initially, Pullman porters were proud of their jobs and were well-respected members of their communities. However, by the end of the 1800s, as younger African American men joined the company and compared their working conditions to those of other Americans, they began to see things differently.

Younger workers objected to their long hours, low salaries, and inferior treatment. An average porter in 1935 worked twice as many hours per week as an American in a manufacturing job. A porter could not collect overtime pay until he had worked 400 hours in a month, yet the company did not count the hours spent preparing and cleaning the train before and after each journey. On average he earned $879 in yearly wages and $237 in tips, but he had to spend $236 for supplies—uniforms, clothes brushes and a shoe-polishing kit. A porter had to purchase daily meals from the dining car, expensive even after a 50% discount, and he was responsible for anything stolen from the train by passengers.

Because their salaries were low, Pullman porters were dependent on tips. They had to please passengers even when the passengers were abusive, hard to satisfy, or made demeaning requests. At a time when thousands of men were looking for jobs, porters who did not meet company standards, unreasonable though they may be, could easily be replaced.

To improve their salaries and working conditions, some porters wanted to organize a union independent of the Pullman Company. These men were spied upon, threatened, and fired. After the Brotherhood of Sleeping Car Porters was finally formed in 1925 under the leadership of Asa Philip Randolph, it had to work hard for ten more years to establish its credibility and gain the support of porters who feared Pullman Company intimidation. When the Brotherhood signed a contract with the company in 1938, it was the first African-American union to sign a labor contract with a major corporation. The Brotherhood had successfully worked to raise salaries to $175 per month, reduce monthly hours from 400 to 240, and ensure job security through the right to a fair hearing. The porters were no longer Pullman's men, but their own.

How does Mr. Lewis show that he's his own man? How does he work for the establishment of the Brotherhood? Explain whether he is a good role model for Bud.

Name _____ **Date** _____

Bud, Not Buddy
Before Reading the Book

Reading Strategy:
Discovering What You Already Know

Reading books is one way of getting information.
Other ways include looking at photographs and illustrations, watching movies and television programs, and listening to the radio and to other people's stories. Think about what you already know about the Great Depression. How did you learn it? Do you know how the Depression changed people's lives? What stories have you heard? Discovering what you already know is like doing a warm-up stretch before exercise. It will make it easier for you to understand and appreciate *Bud, Not Buddy*.

Writing in Your Literature Response Journal

A. **Write about one of these topics in your journal. Circle the topic you chose.**

1. Have you read other novels set during the Great Depression? How were the characters in these stories affected by the Depression? What specific problems did they face? How were their difficulties resolved?

2. Imagine being ten years old and on your own. What problems would you face? How would you solve them? What skills would you need?

3. How are rules and advice different? What rules are you expected to follow? What advice have you been given for being successful and getting along with people? Have you ever made up your own rules or given yourself advice? Give examples.

B. **What were your predictions, questions, observations, and connections about the book? Write about one of them in your journal. Check the response you chose.**

❏ Prediction   ❏ Question   ❏ Observation   ❏ Connection

Literature Circle Guide for Bud, Not Buddy • Scholastic Professional Books

Name _____ Date _____

Bud, Not Buddy
Before Reading the Book

For Your Discussion Group

✳ Like novels, television shows and movies often combine fact and fiction to tell a story that takes place in the past. For instance, the movie *The Patriot* is set in South Carolina during the Revolutionary War, and the television series *Wishbone* is set in different time periods. Make a list of other programs and movies set in the past.

✳ Look through your list. Which titles are based on the lives of real people or on real events? Are audiences looking for information or entertainment when they watch these programs or movies? What do you think the words *docudrama* and *infotainment* mean?

✳ Why might writers or directors make changes to a true story that is made into a book, television show, or movie? Does the writer or director have a responsibility to make sure that a reader or viewer gets accurate information? Or should the reader or viewer be responsible for sorting out fact and fiction?

✳ Why might it be important to know which parts of a story are real and which are made up? Brainstorm a list of strategies you could use to determine which parts of a book, movie, or television program are true. Remember that information about health, science, safety, finance, and cultures, as well as history, might be included.

TIP

When you are brainstorming, remember that the goal is to collect as many different ideas as possible without commenting on them. Everybody's ideas should be included.

Literature Circle Guide for *Bud, Not Buddy* • Scholastic Professional Books

Name _____   **Date** _____

Bud, Not Buddy
Chapters 1–3

Reading Strategy:
First Person Point of View

Look at the first few paragraphs of
Chapter 1. Notice that the narrator,
or person telling the story, uses the
words *we, me, I, my,* and *our*. When
the narrator of the story uses these
first-person pronouns, the story is told from the first-person point of view. You learn not
only what happens to the character, but also what he or she is thinking and feeling.
Keep in mind as you read that the story might be different if it were told from another
character's point of view.

Writing in Your Literature Response Journal

A. Write about one of these topics in your journal. Circle the topic you chose.

1. Write about the events of Chapter 2 from Todd's point of view. Use first-person
pronouns to tell what Todd would be thinking and feeling. How do your feelings
about him change?

2. Bud packs his suitcase when he gets ready to go to the foster home. In it, he puts
his most valuable belongings. Describe what you would put into a small suitcase
if you were headed on a long trip. Explain how you made your decisions.

3. Reread the passage at the end of Chapter 3 in which Bud says that he is mad at
himself for believing in the vampire and getting trapped in the shed. Why does
he blame himself? Who do you think is responsible for the situation in which he
finds himself?

**B. What were your predictions, questions, observations, and connections as you
read? Write about one of them in your journal. Check the response you chose.**

❏ Prediction   ❏ Question   ❏ Observation   ❏ Connection

Literature Circle Guide for *Bud, Not Buddy* • Scholastic Professional Books

Name _____ **Date** _____

Bud, Not Buddy
Chapters 1–3

For Your Discussion Group

✳ Bud said that six is a rough age to be because that is when kids start becoming adults. Brainstorm with your group to develop a definition of *adult*. Is being an adult a matter of age, life experience, or wisdom?

✳ How is being an adult different from being a child? List some typical behaviors of children and adults. What behaviors might indicate that a teenager is moving beyond childhood into adulthood? Does every family and culture have the same expectations for adults and children?

✳ Has Bud handled the problems he's faced as a child or as an adult? Write your answer in your journal. Include examples from the story to back up your opinion. Share your response with the rest of the group.

Writer's Craft: Cliffhangers

Look at the last sentences of Chapters 1-3. Notice that each of them leaves you at an important point in the story and makes you wonder what will happen in the next chapter. Will Bud be happy at his new foster home? What will happen once he's locked in the shed? How will he get his revenge on the Amoses? Final sentences that leave you hanging, that is, leave you wondering what will happen next, are called **cliffhangers**. Like all good writers, Christopher Paul Curtis knows the importance of keeping readers engaged and eager to find out what's going to happen next. Why do you think he ended these chapters with cliffhangers? What other questions do these endings bring to mind?

Name _____   **Date** _____

Bud, Not Buddy
Chapters 4–7

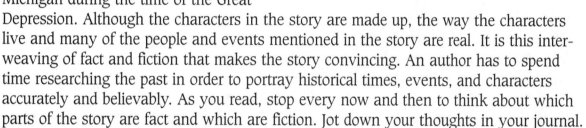

Reading Strategy:
Separating Fact from Fiction

Bud, Not Buddy takes place in the state of
Michigan during the time of the Great
Depression. Although the characters in the story are made up, the way the characters
live and many of the people and events mentioned in the story are real. It is this interweaving of fact and fiction that makes the story convincing. An author has to spend
time researching the past in order to portray historical times, events, and characters
accurately and believably. As you read, stop every now and then to think about which
parts of the story are fact and which are fiction. Jot down your thoughts in your journal.

Writing in Your Literature Response Journal

A. **Write about one of these topics in your journal. Circle the topic you chose.**

1. When Bud enters the Amos house in Chapter 4, he notices their "icebox" and is
surprised that there is "hot water running right into the house." What do his
reactions tell you about his life and about life in general during the 1930s? What
other factual details are woven into the story? Are there any 1930s terms you
don't understand or situations you find confusing?

2. Bud takes revenge on Todd, studies the picture of his mother, meets a "pretend"
family, and goes to the library for help. What do his actions reveal about his
personality? What words describe him best?

3. In Chapter 6, Bud tells how his mom named him. How does his explanation help
us understand why he wants people to call him Bud, not Buddy?

B. **What were your predictions, questions, observations, and connections as you
read? Write about one of them in your journal. Check the response you chose.**

❑ Prediction   ❑ Question   ❑ Observation   ❑ Connection

Literature Circle Guide for *Bud, Not Buddy* • Scholastic Professional Books

Name _____ Date _____

Bud, Not Buddy
Chapters 4–7

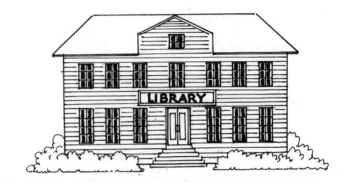

For Your Discussion Group

✻ At the end of Chapter 7, Bud says
  the following:

> *That library door closing after I*
> *walked out was the exact kind of*
> *door Momma had told me about. I knew that since it*
> *had closed the next one was about to open.*

Paraphrase, or put into your own words, what Bud's mom wanted him to know about
doors opening and closing.

✻ Is a door closing always a bad thing? Give examples to support your opinion.

✻ Does Bud know where the next door will lead him? What are his options? Describe his
  attitude. Does he seem to be fearful?

Writer's Craft: Irony

Sometimes people say exactly the opposite of what they mean. For instance, you might
say, "I just *love* cleaning my room" when you actually mean that you don't like to clean
it at all! Such twists in the meaning of words are examples of **irony**. Writers use irony to
grab the attention of readers. Often irony will cause readers to smile or make them think
in a different way.

Situations can also be ironic. In Chapter 6, when Bud's pretend family is waiting in the
food line at the mission, they see a sign that shows a happy, rich, white family riding in
a car. "There's no place like America today!" reads the sign. What is ironic about the picture and its caption? Think about the people looking at the sign and their circumstances.
Do they live in the same America that is pictured on the billboard? What other instances
of irony have you noticed in the book?

Literature Circle Guide for *Bud, Not Buddy* • Scholastic Professional Books

Name _____ **Date** _____

Bud, Not Buddy
Chapter 8

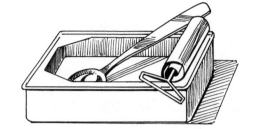

Reading Strategy:
Recognizing Clues in the Text

Chapter 8 is the longest chapter in the book. Flip through the chapter until you find the two breaks or white spaces in the text that break the chapter into three sections. Breaks in the text are like road signs. They indicate that something in the story is changing—perhaps time has passed, the location has changed, or the point of view is switching to another character. For instance, the first part of Chapter 8 takes place in the morning when Bud wakes up; the second part takes place that night when he and Bugs finally get to Hooverville; and the third part takes place the next morning when the train comes through. Paying attention to clues in the text prevents confusion!

Writing in Your Literature Response Journal

A. **Write about one of these topics in your journal. Circle the topic you chose.**

1. Look closely at the three sections in Chapter 8. Try to ignore the breaks as you read these parts of the chapter. Are the breaks necessary? What else might the author have done to indicate the passage of time or a change in location?

2. When Bugs talks about riding the rails on page 62, he says, "*There's always fruits to be picked out west.*" Literally, he means that they can earn enough money to live. But what if *fruits* is read figuratively? What might it symbolize or stand for about life out west? What might the boys want in a new life?

3. Bud obviously wants to be part of a family. Why do you think he feels this way? Doesn't he seem to be getting along pretty well by himself? Deza tells Bud, "*But I guess you're different, aren't you, Bud? I guess you sort of carry your family around inside of you, huh?*" Is she right?

B. **What were your predictions, questions, observations, and connections as you read? Write about one of them in your journal. Check the response you chose.**

❏ Prediction   ❏ Question   ❏ Observation   ❏ Connection

Literature Circle Guide for *Bud, Not Buddy* • Scholastic Professional Books

Name _____   **Date** _____

Bud, Not Buddy
Chapter 8

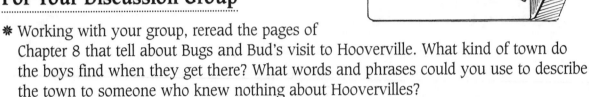

For Your Discussion Group

✻ Working with your group, reread the pages of
Chapter 8 that tell about Bugs and Bud's visit to Hooverville. What kind of town do
the boys find when they get there? What words and phrases could you use to describe
the town to someone who knew nothing about Hoovervilles?

✻ Who lives in Hooverville? Why are they there? How do the residents of Hooverville
manage to live together peacefully? How do they treat one another? What are the
rules of the community, both written and unwritten?

✻ What were your first impressions about life in Hooverville? Did your ideas change by
the time you finished the chapter?

Writer's Craft: Dialogue

As you've been reading *Bud, Not Buddy*, you've probably noticed that the author often
lets the voices of Bud and the people he meets tell the story. Usually their conversations
follow a typical he said-she said pattern, but the conversation between Bud and Bugs
near the beginning of Chapter 8 is different.

I said, "Uh-huh, we kind of had a fight. How long's it take to get out west?"

*Bugs said, "Depends on how many trains you got to hop. Was he really two years
older than you?"*

"Uh-huh, he was twelve. Is it fun to hop a train?"

*"Some of the time it is, some of the time it's scary. We heard he was kind of big too,
was he?"*

Two conversations are really going on at once. Bugs wants to find out about the fight,
and Bud wants to know about riding the rails. Find the whole passage in the book, and
read it aloud with a friend. Notice how the author worked out a pattern of questions and
answers that keeps this complicated conversation from becoming confusing. When
you're writing dialogue, ask friends to read it aloud while you listen and edit.

Literature Circle Guide for Bud, Not Buddy • Scholastic Professional Books

Name _____   **Date** _____

Bud, Not Buddy
Chapters 9–10

Reading Strategy: Making Predictions

What did you think when Bud made his plans to walk 120 miles to Grand Rapids? Did you think something like, "That's too far. He'll never make it!" If you made a prediction, you've picked up one of the habits of a good reader. Developing predictions means that you understand the basics of the story and are thoughtfully evaluating what's going on and why. Always be sure you can supply evidence from the story to support your predictions.

Writing in Your Literature Response Journal

A. Write about one of these topics in your journal. Circle the topic you chose.

1. Think about the events so far in the story. What predictions did you make? Did you expect that Bud would be unhappy in his foster home, that he would take revenge on Todd in a fairly nice way, or that he would try to escape from the man by stealing his car? Have your predictions turned out to be correct? Explain why or why not.

2. What's the difference between knowledge and wisdom? How do you become knowledgeable or wise? In what ways is Bud knowledgeable? Is he wise? Use examples from the story to support your opinion.

3. Bud spends a lot of time in the library. Why does he enjoy it so much? What is your special place? What do you like about it?

B. What were your predictions, questions, observations, and connections as you read? Write about one of them in your journal. Check the response you chose.

❏ Prediction   ❏ Question   ❏ Observation   ❏ Connection

Literature Circle Guide for *Bud, Not Buddy* • Scholastic Professional Books

Name _____ **Date** _____

Bud, Not Buddy
Chapters 9–10

For Your Discussion Group

❋ How did Bud respond when he was
bullied by Billy Burns at the
orphanage? What power did Billy have
over the other kids? What does he
have in common with real-life bullies?

❋ Although Bud doesn't seem very frightened of Billy, he is frightened by the behavior
of the man who stops and offers him a ride. Why is he scared? Read aloud the
passages that support your ideas. What were your first impressions of the man?

❋ There are a lot of funny episodes in *Bud, Not Buddy*. Read aloud your favorites. Talk
about what makes them so enjoyable. Does everyone agree about which passages are
humorous? What makes passages funny to different individuals?

Writer's Craft: Comparisons—Similes and Metaphors

Two kinds of comparisons that help relay complex ideas are **similes** and **metaphors**.
You can identify similes easily because they always begin with the words *like* or *as*. In
Chapter 8, Deza says, "*My momma says these poor kids on the road all alone are like
dust in the wind.*" In Chapter 9, Bud explains why he thinks *ideas are like seeds.*

A metaphor can be more difficult to identify because it does not use signal words such as
like or *as*. A metaphor emphasizes the similarities between two different things. For
example, the librarian who helps Bud says, " . . . *knowledge is a food.*" What does she
mean by that? In order to understand a metaphor, you have to think beyond obvious differences. Think about how food helps you and what happens if you don't have enough.
Think about how knowledge helps you and what happens if you don't have enough.

What other similes or metaphors can you find in *Bud, Not Buddy*? Record them in your
journal. Identify them as similes or metaphors.

Literature Circle Guide for *Bud, Not Buddy* • Scholastic Professional Books

Name _____ **Date** _____

Bud, Not Buddy
Chapters 11–12

Reading Strategy: Drawing Conclusions

Authors don't come right out and tell readers the whole story all at one time. Readers must collect information, look at the evidence the author presents, and draw conclusions about what's happening in the story and why. Sometimes as a story develops, conclusions turn out to be incorrect and must be revised. What conclusions have you reached and revised as you've read this book?

Writing in Your Literature Response Journal

A. Write about one of these topics in your journal. Circle the topic you chose.

1. What conclusions have you been drawing about Bud's search for his father? Will he be successful? Explain your reasoning.

2. Bud collects evidence, but does he always draw the right conclusion? How did he jump to the wrong conclusion about Mr. Lewis?

3. Does Bud's experience with Mr. Lewis remind you of a time when you may have jumped to a conclusion too quickly? Describe what happened.

B. What were your predictions, questions, observations, and connections as you read? Write about one of them in your journal. Check the response you chose.

❏ Prediction ❏ Question ❏ Observation ❏ Connection

Literature Circle Guide for *Bud, Not Buddy* • Scholastic Professional Books

Name _____   **Date** _____

Bud, Not Buddy
Chapters 11–12

For Your Discussion Group

❋ Bud claims to be a good liar. Is he? Does he lie more than he has to? What do you think about his claim that lying to other kids is different from lying to adults? Is Bud right about that?

❋ Compare Kim and Scott Sleet to Todd Amos. How is the Sleet household different from the Amos household? What might account for the differences?

❋ What was your reaction to Mr. Lewis's car being stopped by the policeman? Was Mr. Lewis's attitude the same before and after the stop? Why do you think he is willing to risk carrying the flyers?

❋ Review the comments Mr. Lewis makes about Herman Calloway. Then discuss what your first impressions of Mr. Calloway were.

Writer's Craft: Character Development

What does Mr. Lewis look like? What kind of man is he? If you reread the passages about Mr. Lewis, you'll notice that the author doesn't give us many details about his physical appearance. Neither does Christopher Paul Curtis tell exactly what kind of man Mr. Lewis is. Instead, we see how Mr. Lewis treats Bud and how he interacts with his daughter and her family. The author gives the character's words and shows his actions, and readers draw their own conclusions. In your journal, write about what kind of man you think Mr. Lewis is and what he looks like.

Literature Circle Guide for *Bud, Not Buddy* • Scholastic Professional Books

Name _____   Date _____

Bud, Not Buddy
Chapters 13–15

Reading Strategy: Focusing on Details

If you carefully read the descriptions of the girl's bedroom at the beginning and end of Chapter 15, you can probably draw it from the details the author gives. Details help readers imagine a character's looks and physical surroundings; they also provide clues to a character's personality and behavior. What do you learn about the girl from the description of her room and the things in it?

Writing in Your Literature Response Journal

A. Write about one of these topics in your journal. Circle the topic you chose.

1. Think about the three families Bud has met so far in the story, the Amoses, Deza Malone and her mom, and Mr. Lewis and the Sleets. What are the details that make these families different from one another? Do all the families seem like real families?

2. On page 179, Mr. Calloway says to Bud, "*You've got the rest of them fooled, but not me. There's something about you that I don't like.*" Does he really mean it? What do you think it is about Bud that he doesn't like?

3. After being strong all through the story, why does Bud begin to cry at the end of Chapter 14?

B. What were your predictions, questions, observations, and connections as you read? Write about one of them in your journal. Check the response you chose.

❏ Prediction   ❏ Question   ❏ Observation   ❏ Connection

Literature Circle Guide for *Bud, Not Buddy* • Scholastic Professional Books

Name _____   **Date** _____

Bud, Not Buddy
Chapters 13–15

For Your Discussion Group

❋ Flip through the book and make a list of "Bud's Rules and Things." Are his rules useful? What rules would you add to help him get along in his present situation?

❋ Mr. Calloway locked the closet doors in Bud's bedroom. How does that fit in with Bud's theory that when one door closes, another opens?

❋ Do the characters seem real, or are they stereotypes? Are the women all kind and loving like Miss Thomas and the men gruff and unfeeling like Mr. Calloway?

Writer's Craft: Euphemisms

Rules and Things Number 28
Gone = dead!

Sometimes, when the feelings attached to a word are unpleasant or very strong, we choose to use another word instead. *Dead* is one of those words. Often you will hear people say *at rest*, *passed on*, *expired*, or *deceased* in its place. Other examples of euphemisms are *intoxicated*, *stout,* and *senior citizen*. Which words do they replace?

Bud seems to have no patience for euphemisms. Explain whether you agree or disagree with him.

Literature Circle Guide for *Bud, Not Buddy* • Scholastic Professional Books

Name _____ Date _____

Bud, Not Buddy
Chapters 16–18

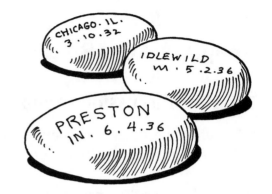

Reading Strategy:
Identifying Confusing Parts

As the story comes to a close, be sure you
understand what's going on. If you get to
a section that confuses you, look back
through the chapter until you find the last section you understood completely. Read
through the confusing section again and try to diagnose the problem. Are there unfamil-
iar words or phrases? Did you lose track of who was speaking? Are the sentences long
and complex? Often identifying a problem goes a long way towards solving it. If you run
into a confusing passage that really stumps you, discuss it with your group.

Writing in Your Literature Response Journal

A. Write about one of these topics in your journal. Circle the topic you chose.

1. What causes you to get lost when you're reading? What is your strategy for
getting back into the story? Write about the passages in *Bud, Not Buddy* you've
found confusing.

2. Do you think Mr. Calloway is mistreating Bud? Why is Bud happy with his
situation? In what ways is his life better than it was before?

3. You've probably noticed that the band members freely tease and joke with one
another. What's the tone or feeling of their discussion at the beginning of Chapter
18? How does the segregated society of the time show in their work and their
dealings with one another?

B. What were your predictions, questions, observations, and connections as you
read? Write about one of them in your journal. Check the response you chose.

❏ Prediction ❏ Question ❏ Observation ❏ Connection

Literature Circle Guide for *Bud, Not Buddy* • Scholastic Professional Books

Name _____ **Date** _____

Bud, Not Buddy
Chapters 16–18

For Your Discussion Group

✳ Did you expect that Mr. Calloway would turn out to be Bud's grandfather? What hints did the author provide? Clear up any confusion by referring back to Chapters 12-18.

✳ What does Miss Thomas mean when she tells Bud on page 191, *"Something tells me you were a godsend to us, you keep that in mind all of the time, OK"*? Do you agree with her? Why should Bud always remember that?

✳ Bud's been very particular about his name. Why do you suppose he's so happy to have the band give him a nickname?

Writer's Craft: Foreshadowing

In Chapter 8, after Bud misses the train that was to take him to the West, he looks at the blue flyer and notices the similarities between his name, Caldwell, and Calloway, the name of the man on the flyer. This is an example of **foreshadowing**, the hints a clever author gives readers about what might happen later in the story. Sometimes it takes a second reading to identify clues. Skim through the parts of the story about Bud's family and make note of other details that foreshadow future events in the story.

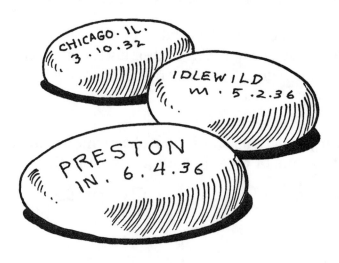

Literature Circle Guide for *Bud, Not Buddy* • Scholastic Professional Books

Name _____ Date _____

Bud, Not Buddy
Chapter 19 and Afterword

Reading Strategy:
Understanding an Author's Purpose

Sometimes you have to read between the lines to figure out what the author is trying to tell you. But in some books, an author's message is spelled out in the beginning of a book in a preface, introduction, or foreword or at the end in an afterword. What do you learn in the Afterword about Christopher Paul Curtis's purpose for writing *Bud, Not Buddy*? How does that information affect your feelings about the book?

Writing in Your Literature Response Journal

A. Write about one of these topics in your journal.
Circle the topic you chose.

1. Summarize what Christopher Paul Curtis says to his readers in the Afterword. Did reading about his family and their part in his novel change your feelings about the story? What was your response to the photographs?

2. Looking at the evidence in the story, describe the relationship between Bud's mom and her father. What might have caused their estrangement? Were they both happy about the separation? If not, why did it last so long?

3. Despite all that happens to Bud, there only seem to be a few times when he is uneasy or afraid. How do you account for this?

B. What were your predictions, questions, observations, and connections as you read? Write about one of them in your journal. Check the response you chose.

❏ Prediction ❏ Question ❏ Observation ❏ Connection

Literature Circle Guide for *Bud, Not Buddy* • Scholastic Professional Books

Name _____ **Date** _____

Bud, Not Buddy
Chapter 19 and Afterword

For Your Discussion Group

✷ Think about where Bud was when the story started and where he is at the end. What enabled him to survive? Was it luck, skill, or something else?

✷ The author tells us in the Afterword that some story ideas for the novel came from his family and other parts grew from his imagination and research. Can you identify which parts of the story came from each source? Are there parts of the story you're not sure about? Do the different parts blend successfully?

✷ Racism plays an essential, but subtle role in this story. How did it affect you as you were reading? Were you aware that most of the characters were African American? What would the story be missing without the element of race in it?

Writer's Craft: Developing Story Ideas

Sometimes developing an idea for a story is the hardest part of writing. Next time, do what Christopher Paul Curtis did. Let your story grow from the people you know. Interview them about their lives, and do some library research to fill in the details.

Good questions to ask in an interview are open-ended and require an extended answer. "When were you born" will only earn a short answer. "Tell me about your school years" will draw out more. You can always follow up with specific questions to fill in the gaps. Take a moment to think of someone who has an interesting life. Write a set of open-ended questions you might ask him or her.

Literature Circle Guide for *Bud, Not Buddy* • Scholastic Professional Books

Name _____ **Date** _____

Bud, Not Buddy
After Reading

An author carries out his or her purpose by developing themes or important ideas in a story. Reflect on what you've read. What does Christopher Paul Curtis want you to remember about families, survival, hope, and opportunity?

✻ Begin by writing your ideas individually. Feel free to go back to the story and check your journal writings to refresh your memory. As a group, work together to combine your ideas and develop a statement about each theme.

✻ Sometimes when you finish reading a novel, there is unfinished business. You might have a good idea about what happened to the characters *before* and *during* the story, but you're left wondering what might happen to them *after* the story.

✻ Think about the following questions:

1. Will Bud's life with his grandfather be a happy one? Will Bud actually turn out to be a godsend to his grandfather as Miss Thomas predicted?

2. What part will the band, Miss Thomas, and music play in Bud's new life?

3. How will Herman Calloway feel about having his grandson in his life? How will he treat Bud?

✻ How do you think Bud's life will be affected by each person or thing in the first column of the chart? Predict what might happen in a sequel to *Bud, Not Buddy*. Reproduce the chart below on a large sheet of paper, and use it to record your predictions.

	Prediction:	**Evidence from the story:**
Herman E. Calloway		
Miss Thomas		
The Band		
Music		

Literature Circle Guide for *Bud, Not Buddy* • Scholastic Professional Books

Individual Projects

1. If you've enjoyed reading *Bud, Not Buddy*, you might also enjoy other award-winning books about foster children, such as *The Pinballs* by Betsy Byars and *The Great Gilly Hopkins* by Katherine Paterson. Two good novels about doors opening and closing are *A Door in the Wall* by Marguerite D'Angeli and *The Big Bazoohley* by Peter Carey. As you read these books, note how two authors may start with a similar idea but develop it differently.

2. Start a folder of favorite passages from the books you read. Skim through the chapters of *Bud, Not Buddy* that you most enjoyed. Copy three or four sections that made you think, laugh, or imagine something new. Do the same for other books. Include the title of the book and page number of each passage.

3. Bud carefully studied the blue flyer and the picture of his mother for clues about his family. Examine a few photographs of people in your family. What can you learn about them and the way they lived? What questions come to mind as you study the pictures? Are there any objects you can study in the same way that Bud looked at his collections of flyers and rocks?

Group Projects

1. Check books and Web sites for photographs from the 1930s that could illustrate scenes from *Bud, Not Buddy* or show people's daily lives. Look especially for pictures of children, Hoovervilles, Big Bands, breadlines and soup kitchens, strikes, and Pullman porters.

2. Check an encyclopedia for three or four important facts about the people, places and events mentioned in the story—John Brown; Al Capone; George Washington Carver; Ruth Dandridge; Pretty Boy Floyd; J. Edgar Hoover; Baby Face Nelson; Satchel Paige; Allen Pinkerton; Flint, Michigan, labor organizations; Pullman porters; Redcaps; unions; and strikes. Gather your findings into an illustrated booklet that can become part of your classroom library, or develop a web page or PowerPoint presentation to share with the rest of your class.

3. Look at the questions in the After Reading section on the previous page. Using one of the questions as a springboard, write a scene that might appear in a sequel to *Bud, Not Buddy*.

Literature Circle Guide for *Bud, Not Buddy* • Scholastic Professional Books